Sam's Dental Adventure

A child's first exploration of the dental world

Asmeen Hossenboccus and Dr Moniba Khan

Illustrator: Nabeel Tahir

Grosvenor House
Publishing Limited

This book is published by
Grosvenor House Publishing Ltd
Link House
140 The Broadway, Tolworth, Surrey, KT6 7HT.
www.grosvenorhousepublishing.co.uk

A CIP record for this book
is available from the British Library

Paperback ISBN: 978-1-80381-279-3
Hardback ISBN: 978-1-80381-278-6

For our darling angels Grace, Bahaa, Omar and Jemima
and the women who have inspired us:
our beautiful mothers Asmat and Jabeen.

Sam's mummy puts on some washing up gloves and places a mask over her mouth. Sam can't stop giggling.

"Hello, Sam!" said Mummy, "I'm your dentist!"

"Hello Dentist!" Sam replied, he was so excited to be role-playing with his mummy!

"Hop onto this chair for me," instructed Mummy.

Sam sits down on the chair. "Open your mouth wide,
like a lion!" said Mummy.
Sam chuckles and opens his mouth WIDE. "ROAR!" he said.
Using a teaspoon, Mummy pretends to check Sam's teeth.
"What's that, Mummy?" asked Sam. "Does the dentist use a spoon?"

"No, dentists have a special little mirror that
helps them see inside your mouth."

"Goodness me, what a big mouth you have!" said Mummy.
"Mummy!" said Sam whilst laughing.
Mummy began to chuckle too. "So, you'll sit like this in
the big chair that moves up and down, so the dentist can look
into your mouth without needing to bend or stretch.
Okay, it's your turn to check my teeth now!"

"Yay!" Sam was excited to play the role of the dentist.
Sam used another teaspoon to check his mummy's teeth.

"How many teeth do I have Sam?"
Sam gently tapped against his mummy's teeth and shouted,
"Wow! You have 32 teeth Mummy!"

Sam and Mummy made their way to their first dental visit!
Sam looked up at the big shiny gold letters.
"We're here Sam, SMILE SPA! Doesn't it look wonderful?"

SMILE SPA

OPEN

Sam and his mummy walk inside and are greeted by a lovely smiley lady at reception.
"We have an appointment at 3 o'clock."
"Yes, hello! Please take a seat, we will call you in just a moment," said the receptionist.

While sitting in the waiting room, Sam notices a lot of people: old, young and even a gurgling baby.

Then he notices someone sitting next to him. Someone his own age. "Hello, my name is Jasmine. I ate too many sweets so I'm here to see my dentist. What are you here for?" She smiles at Sam and he notices her teeth are brown and she has a couple of teeth missing!

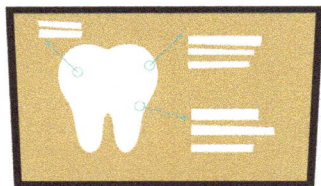

WAITING ROOM

Sam gasps, "I'm here to see the dentist for the very first time."
"Great! Everyone here is very nice." Says Jasmine.

WAITING ROOM

ASMAT NURSE

A nurse dressed in white appears and calls out, "Jasmine next, please."
Jasmine and her dad get up and hurry off to see the dentist.

"Sam next please."
Sam and his mummy go into the dentist's room
and Sam begins to look all around.
There is a big chair in the middle of the room,
which is under a bright shiny light.
The entire room looks and smells so clean.

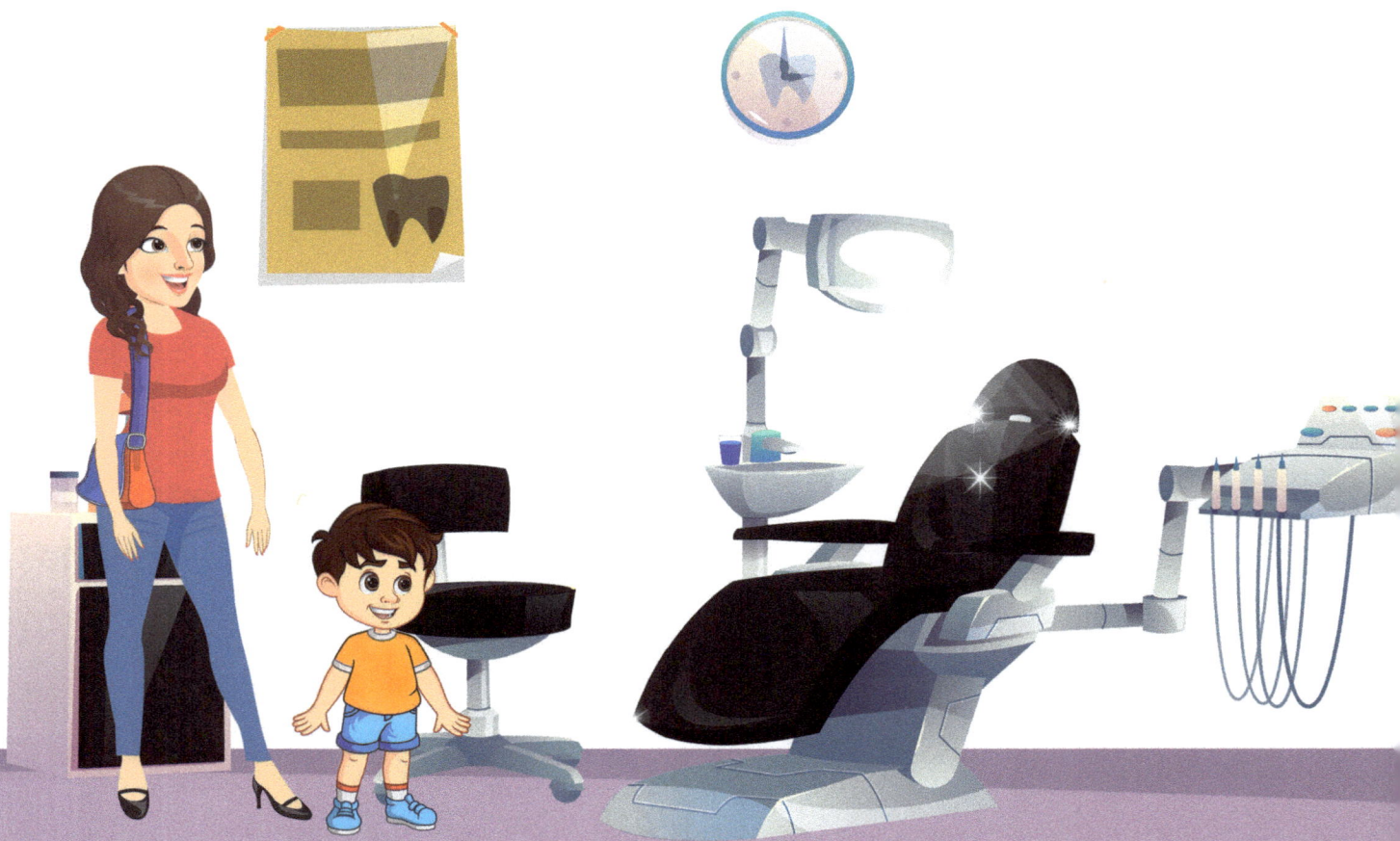

"Hello, I'm Moniba, your dentist."
Sam smiles back at Moniba, "Hello!"
Moniba shows Sam how the chair works, raising and
lowering it and tilting it backwards and forwards.
"It's like a funfair ride!" said Moniba, who then winked at Sam.
Sam burst into laughter. He was having so much fun!

Moniba then explains how she is going to check and count Sam's teeth with a small round mirror.

"It's to make sure they're all there!" she said with a smile. Sam puts on the bib and glasses and is now ready for his first dental check-up!

"Remember... open wide like a lion!" said Mummy. "RRRRWWWWOOOOAAARRRRR!"

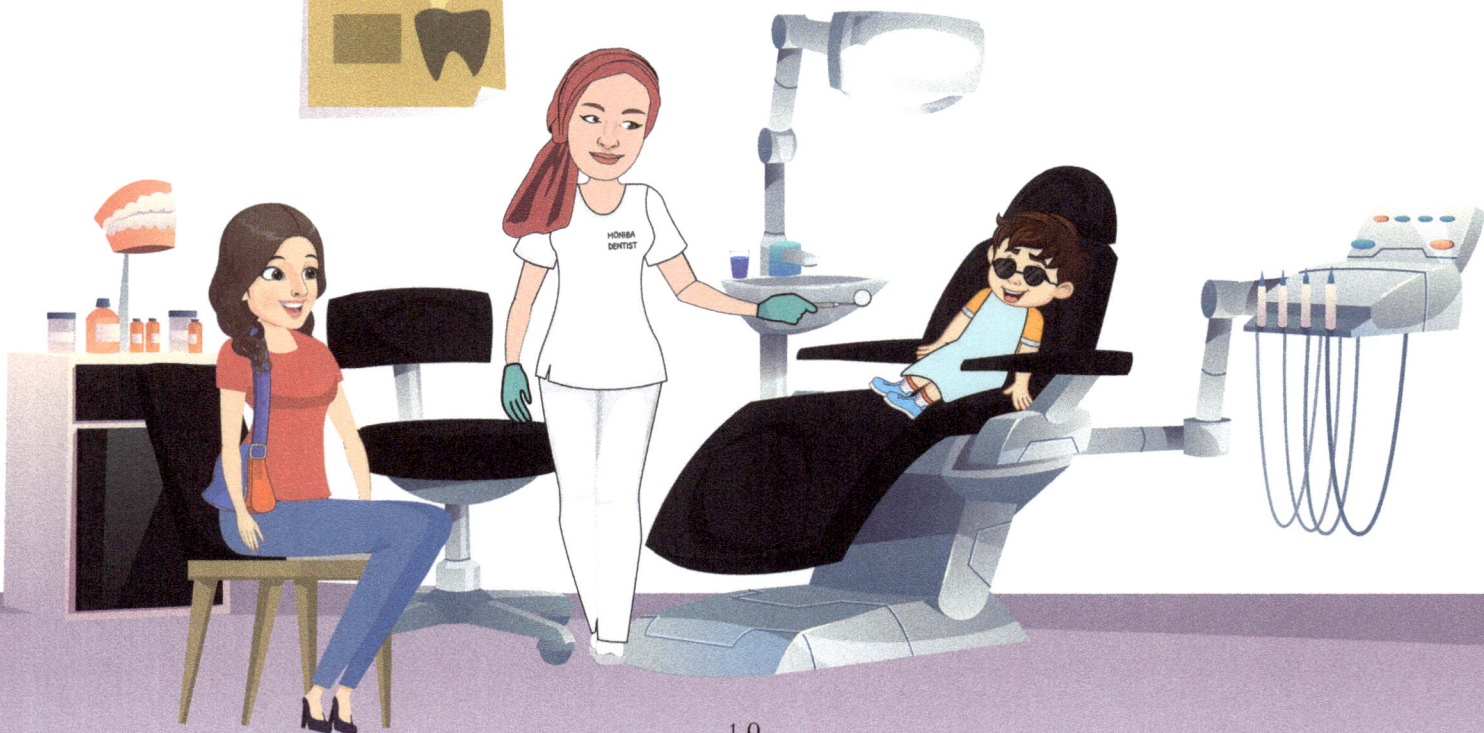

Moniba gives Sam a little round mirror with a long handle. It looks as long as a toothbrush. She then shows Sam the air blower which helps to dry the teeth so the dentist can see better. Moniba also has a little pointy stick to tickle Sam's tooth.

"Oh!" said Moniba, "You have a small hole in this tooth."

11

"Why is there a hole?" said Sam.
"Maybe you've had too much sugar or not brushed properly?" replied Moniba. "We need to put a little bandage on this tooth."
Moniba explains to Sam and his mummy what will happen next.

Moniba shows Sam the suction machine which is like a gentle hoover. She also showed Sam the whizzy tools. Moniba filled the hole in Sam's tooth and then asks Sam to rinse his mouth with the blue liquid next to the chair.

"Remember my dear, spit it out and don't drink it." Sam spits out the blue liquid into the little sink beside the chair turning the whole sink blue.

Moniba hands a diet sheet to Mummy so she can write down all the food and drinks Sam has on two weekdays and one weekend. "Only have sugary foods at mealtimes and no sticky sweets. Juice has a lot of sugar in it so try to only drink water: it's the best drink!"

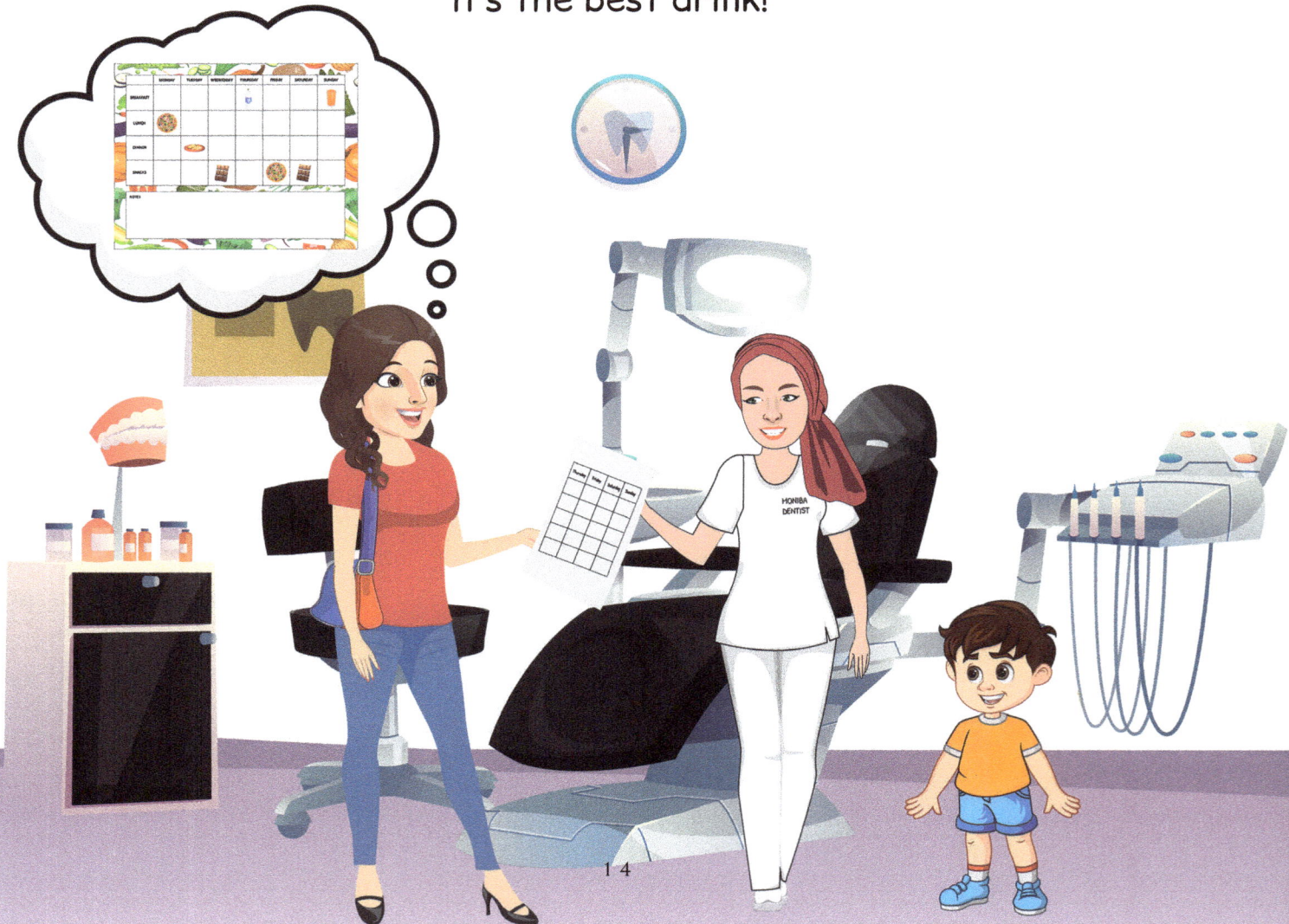

Sam then follows the nurse to the hygienist's room.
"Well, hello there!" said Asmeen, with a big smile.
"I'm Asmeen, your hygienist. Jump on the chair for me.
So, tell me, what do you think a dental hygienist does?"
Sam thought for a moment. "Well, hygiene means being
clean...So, are you a special mouth cleaner?"

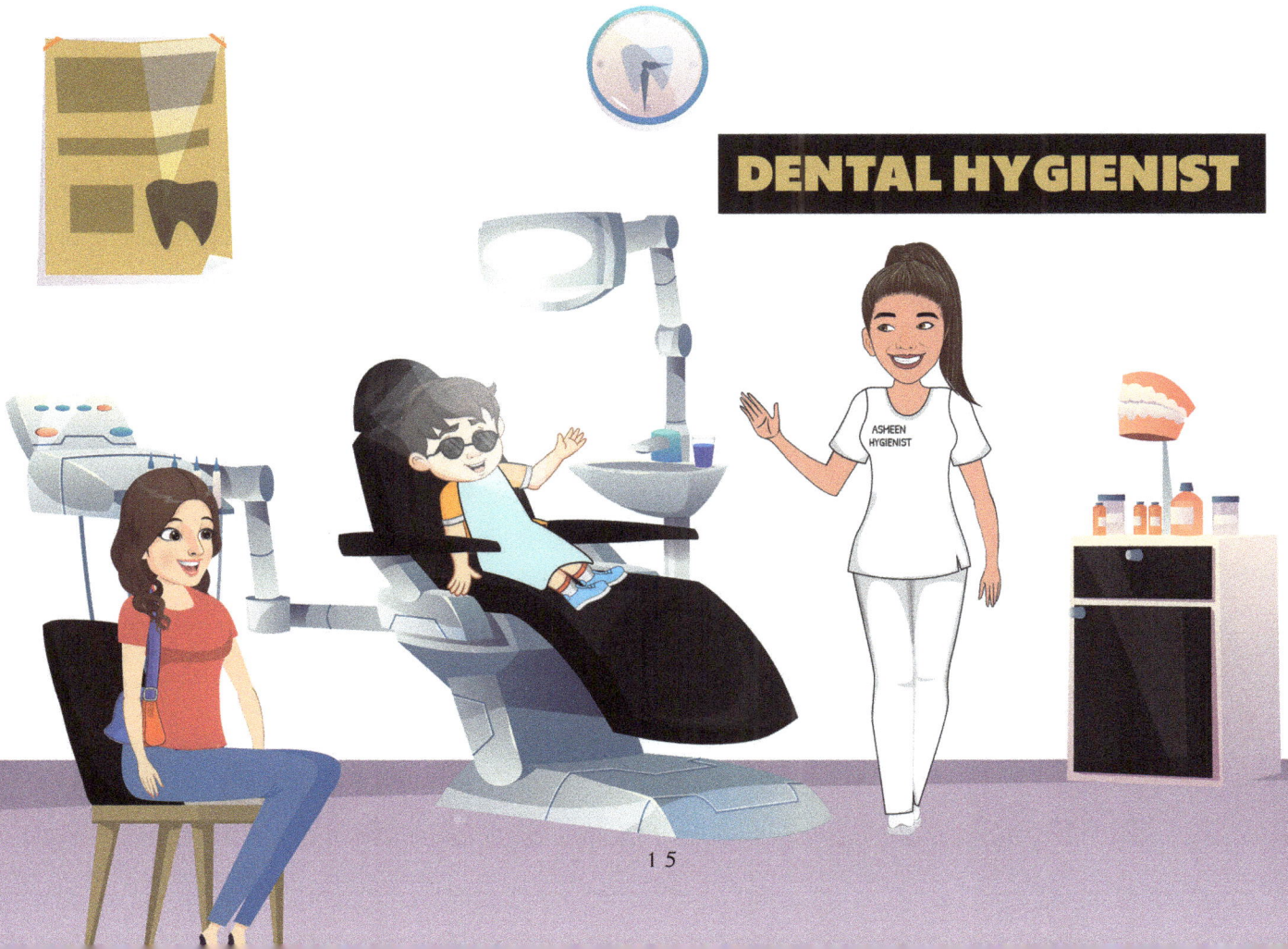

DENTAL HYGIENIST

ASHEEN
HYGIENIST

"Very clever!" Said Asmeen. "I will give your teeth a good sparkly clean. But first, let me teach you about germs on your teeth. Here, chew on this pink tablet. If you have any germs it will go bright purple! How cool is that?"

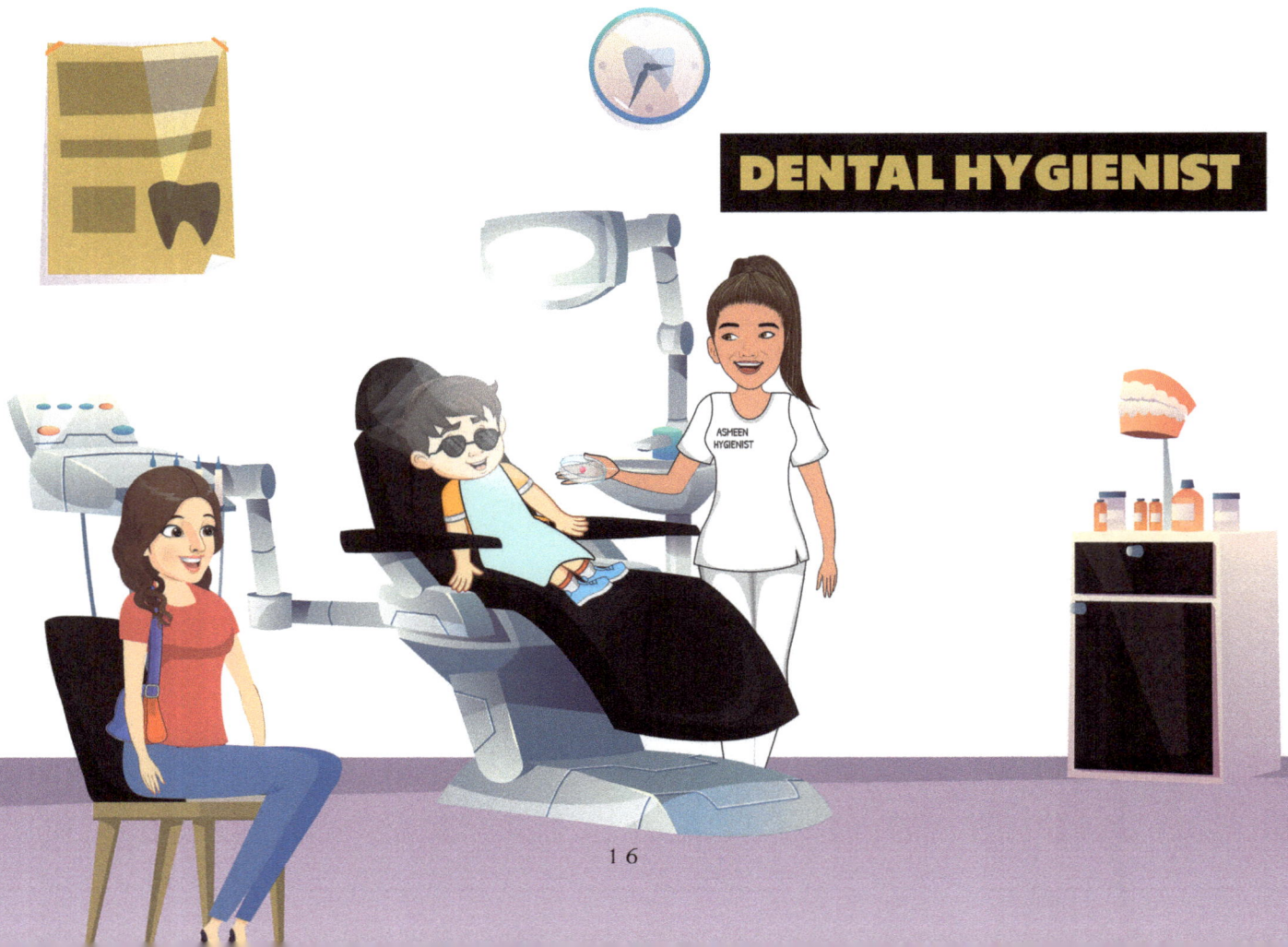

DENTAL HYGIENIST

ASMEEN HYGIENIST

Sam looked in the mirror and could see lots
of purple where he needed to brush better.
Asmeen used a model to show Sam how to brush properly.
"Remember to brush: OUTSIDE, INSIDE and ON TOP,
once in the morning and
once at night."

DENTAL H

Asmeen cleaned Sam's teeth with her special tools and asked him to rinse his mouth out.
"Now it's polishing time!" Asmeen said excitedly.
"What flavour paste would you like?"
"Strawberry please!" said Sam.
Asmeen began polishing his teeth.
"That tickles!" laughed Sam.
When Asmeen was finished, Sam's teeth looked shiny and felt squeaky clean!

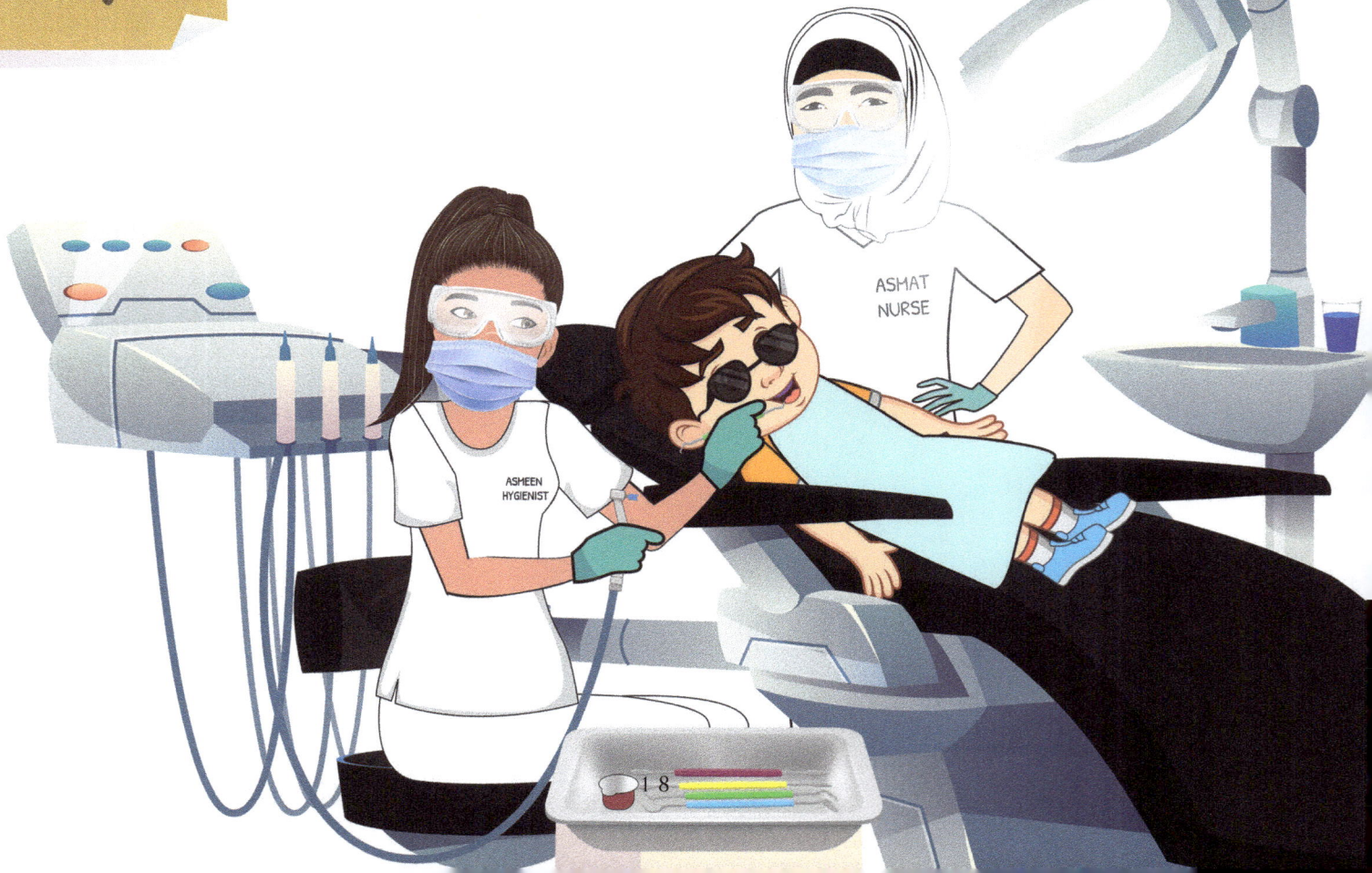

Asmeen explained how Fluoride in toothpaste
helps to keep your teeth nice and strong.
"Remember at the end of brushing, spit and don't rinse.
That's it, you're all done for today! Except..."
"Except for what?" asked Sam, curiously.
"STICKERS! You did amazing Sam, well done!"

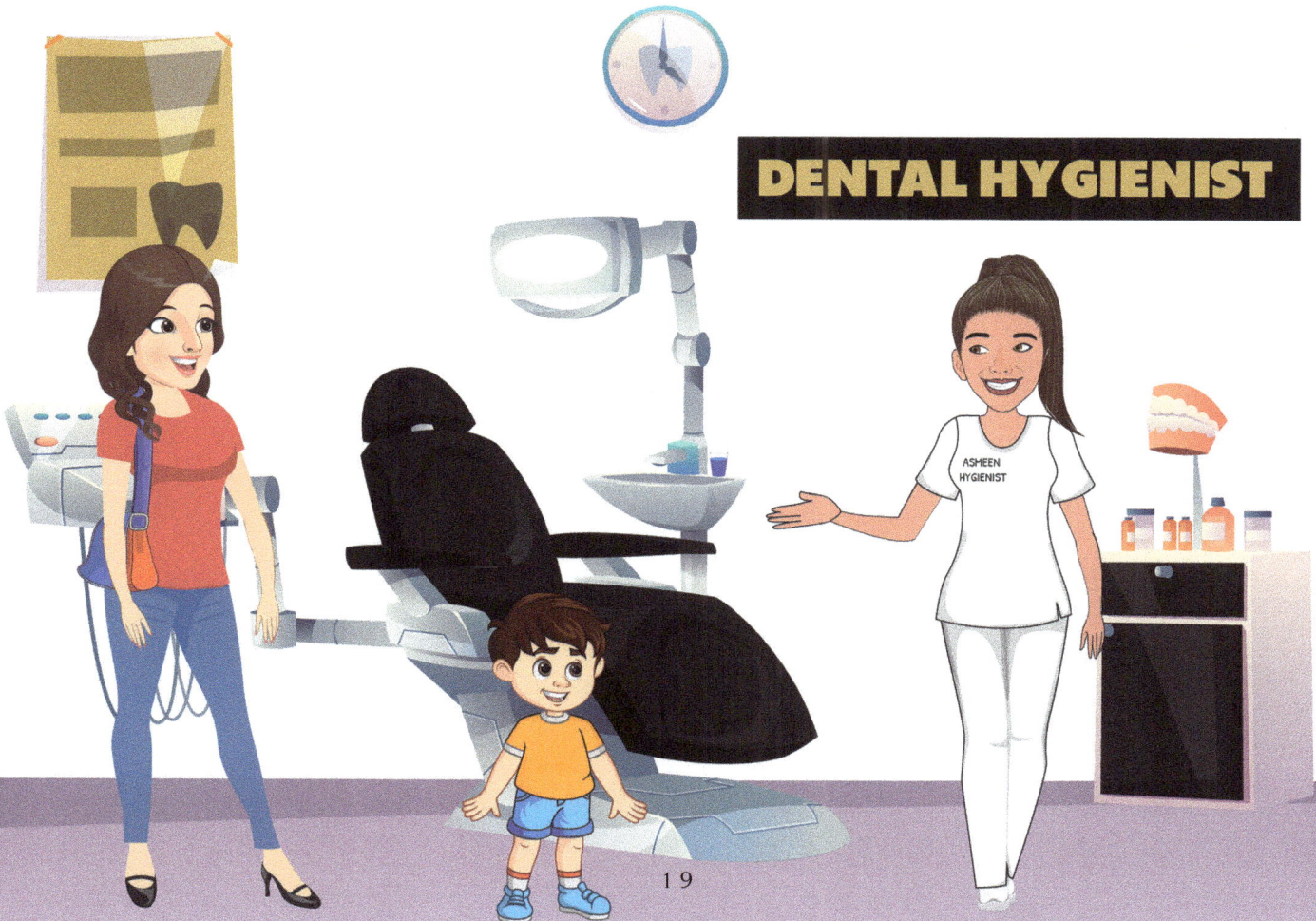

DENTAL HYGIENIST

ASMEEN
HYGIENIST

19

Sam and Mummy make their way to reception
to collect his sticker and to book in his next
visit in six months' time.
"Yay!" said Sam, as he chose a sticker of a tooth hero
and proudly put it on his jumper straight away.
On their way home, Sam said, "That was fun Mummy!
I can't wait to come back again!"

The next day, Sam arrived at school and ran to
see his friends Grace, Bahaa, Omar and Jemima.
He showed off his sticker, smiled and said, "I can't wait
to tell you all about my first dental adventure!"

About the authors:
Asmeen Hossenboccus

Asmeen is used to being unique: she is half Mauritian, quarter Pakistani and quarter Malaysian! An avid charity fundraiser and former army cadet, Asmeen is energetic, ambitious and driven, counterbalanced with a sense of fun and love of adventure! Her ambition is to own a chain of dental practices or 'hygiene hubs' something she is working towards whilst currently studying for her Masters' in Business Administration (MBA). She holds qualifications from world-renowned universities including her BSc degree in Biomedical Science from Kings College London and her Diplomas in Dental Hygiene and Therapy from UCL Eastman Dental Institute qualifying from the Royal College of Surgeons, England.

Asmeen has twin boys Omar and Bahaa, and enjoys an especially close relationship with her mum, Asmat. When she is not working, studying, writing or being a mum, she spends time with friends and family, travelling, dancing and reading/listening to audiobooks. She is also dedicated to charity work both locally and internationally; helping in refugee camps, building water wells, schools, orphanages, birthing clinics and feeding the homeless.

Asmeen's passion for helping others can also be seen in her writing: her adult work in progress is a self-help, positive and motivational book, whilst this children's book, dedicated to her mum and twins, is aimed at helping children acclimatise to the dental environment and to understand not just role of the dentist, but uniquely the role of the dental hygienist too.

About the authors:
Moniba Khan

Moniba is a free spirit, a chocolate brownie entrepreneur and a dentist! Passionate about helping others, she has provided dental care and treatment to refugees in camps, including those on the Greek island of Lesbos. Moniba graduated in 2011 from the prestigious dental school, King's College London. She has a special interest in Restorative and Aesthetic dentistry, enabling her to enhance her patients' smiles. She has a wonderful and supportive husband, Mohamed and they have two beautiful daughters, Grace and Jemima, as well as a cat, Mia: a British shorthair who rules the roost!

The chocolate brownie company, called Sweetooth Brownies, was on international sensation, featured in the pages of British Vogue with sales sending the brownies all over the world. A strange side-line for a dentist, perhaps, but Moniba understands the power of a sweet tooth, as evidenced by the name of the company!

Moniba's writing is inspired by her children and her life. She has dedicated this book to her beautiful daughters in hope they will aspire to do and be the best they can be in life, with a positive mindset and a good attitude, anything is possible; including overcoming your fear of visiting the dentist! Moniba has written this book to demonstrate how positive encouragement, good words, mental preparation and a good mind set can help you to overcome any hurdle.

When not tending to other people's teeth, Moniba likes to travel with her husband and children and cherish every moment together.

Follow @asmeen.smiles and @sweetoothbrownies for all the latest teeth tips!

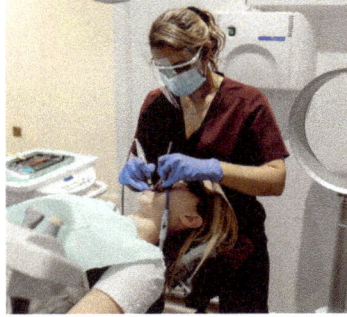

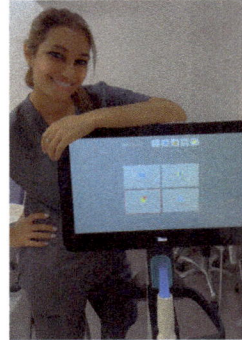

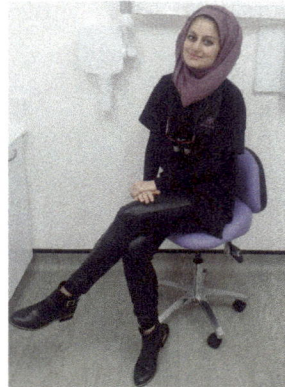

Colour me in!

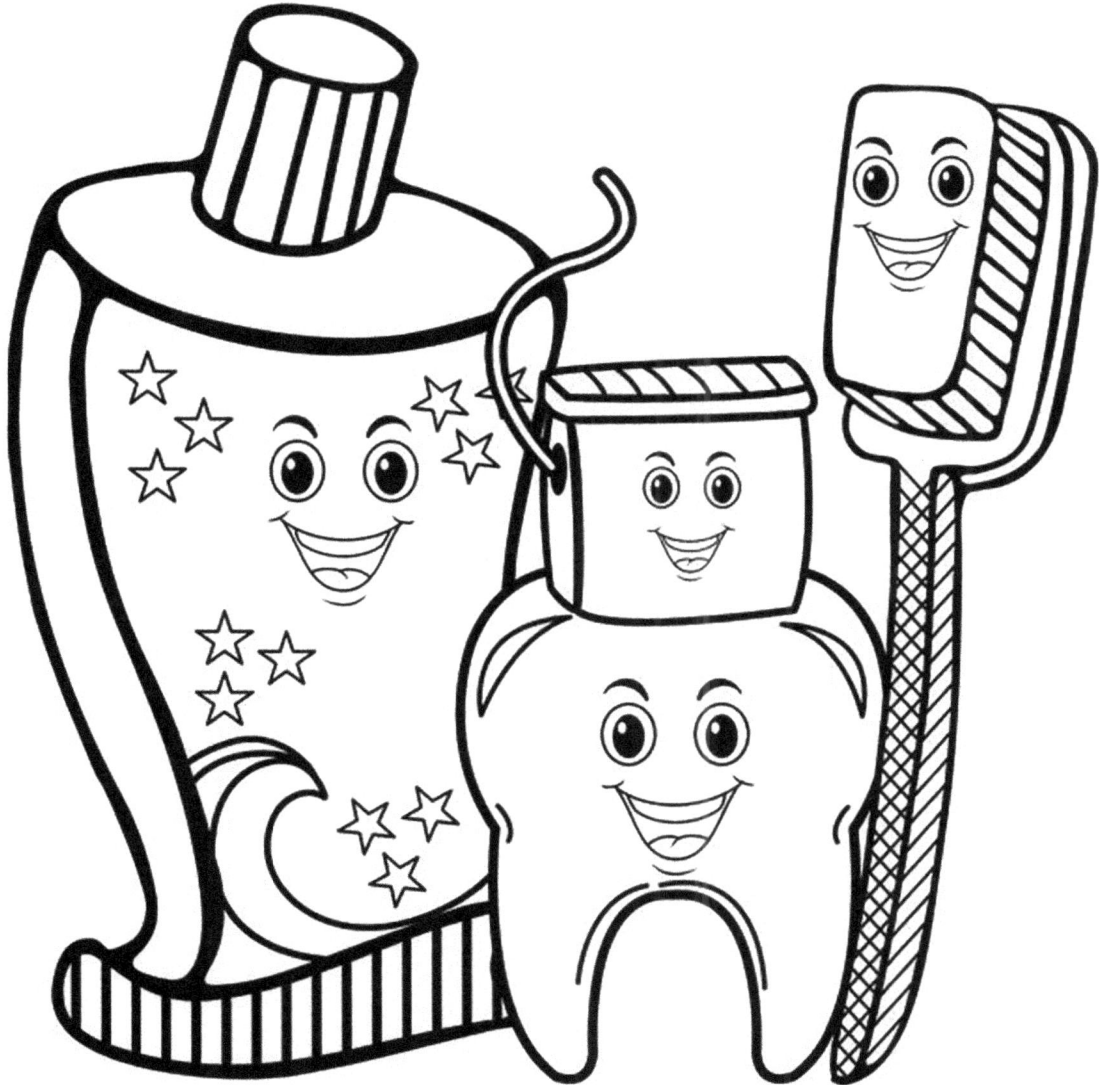

www.ingramcontent.com/pod-product-compliance
Lightning Source LLC
Chambersburg PA
CBHW041435040426
42452CB00023B/2985